Just Sell It: Easy Guide to Selling Online and Offline

Discover the Secret Strategies that Help a First-Time Entrepreneur Make Thousands in Sales

By Rafael AG Jr.

Rafael.Gutierrezjr@gmail.com

Instagram: https://www.instagram.com/ralf206

https://TuOpinion.org

COPYRIGHT

No part of this eBook may be reproduced or transmitted in any form or by any means, electronic or mechanical, including photocopying, recording or by any information storage and retrieval system, without written permission from the author.

This document is geared towards providing exact and reliable information in regards to the topic and issue covered. The publication is sold with the idea that the publisher is not required to render accounting, officially permitted, or otherwise, qualified services. If advice is necessary, legal or professional, a practiced individual in the profession should be ordered.

- From a Declaration of Principles which was accepted and approved equally by a Committee of the American Bar Association and a Committee of Publishers and Associations.

In no way is it legal to reproduce, duplicate, or transmit any part of this document in either electronic means or in printed format. Recording of this publication is strictly prohibited and any storage of this document is not allowed unless with written permission from the publisher. All rights reserved.

The information provided herein is stated to be truthful and consistent, in that any liability, in terms of inattention or otherwise, by any usage or abuse of any policies, processes, or directions contained within is the solitary and utter responsibility of the recipient reader. Under no circumstances will any legal responsibility or blame be held against the publisher for any reparation, damages, or monetary loss due to the information herein, either directly or indirectly.

Respective authors own all copyrights not held by the publisher.

The information herein is offered for informational purposes solely, and is universal as so. The presentation of the information is without contract or any type of guarantee assurance.

The trademarks used are without any consent, and the publication of the trademark is without permission or backing by the trademark owner. All trademarks and brands within this book are for clarifying purposes only and are owned by the owners themselves, and are not affiliated with this document.

LEGAL DISCLAIMERS

The information provided within this Book is for general informational purposes only. While we try to keep the information up-to-date and correct, there are no representations or warranties, express or implied, about the completeness, accuracy, reliability, suitability or availability with respect to the information, products, services, or related graphics contained in this eBook for any purpose. Any use of this information is at your own risk.

The methods describe within this Book are the author's personal thoughts. They are not intended to be a definitive set of instructions for this project. You may discover there are other methods and materials to accomplish the same end result.

The information contained within this eBook is strictly for educational purposes. If you wish to apply ideas contained in this eBook, you are taking full responsibility for your actions.

The author has made every effort to ensure the accuracy of the information within this book was correct at time of publication. The author does not assume and hereby disclaims any liability to any party for any loss, damage, or disruption caused by errors or omissions, whether such errors or omissions result from accident, negligence, or any other cause.

Cover Illustration Copyright © 2018 by Rafael AG Jr.

Publication Date: May 2019

Editing by Teressa J. Parker

Updated legal disclaimers and copyright at https://TuOpinion.org

ACKNOWLEDGEMENTS

This book is based on Just Sell It: Easy Guide to Selling Online and Offline. And this work would not have the spirit it has without the invaluable academic, educational, psychological, and human support and belief in me as a writer and researcher.

I have provided you with meaningful information and strategies on on how and where to sell your products; to help you understand better, create more balance and fulfilment in all areas of your business (small, medium or large). Don't miss it!

Firstly, my profound gratitude and sincere thanks to Almighty God for His support and guidance through out the research. His continued support led me to the right way.

I would also like to extend my indebtedness to my family for their advice during my research. Without their encouragement, I would not have a chance to complete this book.

And to my friends and co-workers, I acknowledge my heartfelt for their valuable guidance, constant encouragement, and untiring help which has been a source of inspiration at all stages of the work.

As a way of showing my appreciation to God over the accomplishment of this book, after the sales of this book, I am helping the a non-profit organization financially with 30% of any income generated.

Contents

COPYRIGHT	2
LEGAL DISCLAIMERS	4
ACKNOWLEDGEMENTS	6
ABOUT THE AUTHOR	10
INTRODUCTION	12
A GOOD PHOTO SELLS, BUT A GREAT PHOTO SELLS MORE	16
THE POWER OF VIDEO	18
INCLUDE POWERFUL WORDS TO INCREASE SALES	20
SELLING YOUR PRODUCT ON AMAZON	22
HOW TO BOOST SALES ON AMAZON	25
INCREASING YOUR CONVERSION RATE ON AMAZON	32
INCREASE SALES AND CONVERSION RATES WITH ZEN CART	34
INCREASE YOUR SALES USING THIS SHOPPING CART TIP	41
SELLING ON EBAY	43
SMARTPHONE APPS THAT SELL	47
INTRODUCTION TO DROP SHIPPING	58
THE CLEAR ADVANTAGES OF DROP SHIPPING	58
HOW CAN BUSINESS OWNERS OFFER DROP SHIPPING TO INCREASE SALES	61
BENEFITS OF DROP SHIPPING	68
HOW TO GET YOUR PRODUCT INTO WALMART AND TARGET	71
HOW TO GET YOUR PRODUCT INTO TARGET	85
HOW TO SUBMIT PRODUCT TO TARGET	90
GOVERNMENT CONTRACTING	100

GOVERNMENT CONTRACT PROPOSAL WRITING TIPS	104
GUIDES FOR OBTAINING GSA CONTRACTS	117
HOW TO GET A GSA SCHEDULE CONTRACT AND SELL TO THE GOVERNMENT	120
HOW TO WIN A GOVERNMENT CONTRACT	127
SUMMARY	134

ABOUT THE AUTHOR

Rafael A. Gutierrez Jr. is a former US Marine and a prolific Entreprenuer and Finance & Business Director whose unparalleled reliability, ambition, dedication have all earned him the reputation as a seasoned leader across Orange County, California. Over the course of a decade, he has garnered extensive finance and accounting industry experience. In addition to finance and accounting, he is well-versed in management, financial analysis, budget development & management, cash flow forecasting, taxes, payroll, financial modeling, P&L analysis, project management, and various other specialty areas.

An entrepreneurial spirit with an unshakable drive for as long as he can remember, Rafael now spearheads three different lucrative business ventures. Currently, he proudly serves as the Owner of Viajway Luggage and the President of Monte Cristi Capital Group.

Rafael was also the Finance & Business Director at a local non-profit organization, where he strategically developed top-tier financial strategies and closely analyzed present reports and forthcoming financial activities. Prior to that, Business Manager at a career school, and the President of the Toastmasters Club in Buena Park from 2010 to 2014.

Furthermore, Rafael holds a B.S. degree in Financial Management and an M.S. degree in Corporate & International Finance from National University. He is currectly attending the University of the People for a B.S. in Computer Science.

When he isn't immersed in his multifaceted career, you can find Rafael traveling across the globe, relaxing at the beach, or hiking in the great outdoors. He also enjoys attending baseball games and live music events. Above all, he is an avid reader and lifelong learner.

If you are interested in his services or would like to network with him, feel free to reach out to Rafael A. Gutierrez Jr. directly at Rafael.GutierrezJr@gmail.com.

INTRODUCTION

Are you interested in selling like nobody else? Want to take ownership of your future, and build a valuable asset you can grow into a profitable, scalable business?

Perhaps you want to obtain a GSA contract, or win a government contract. If any of this applies to you, you are in the right place!

You created this amazing product, and you thought as soon as you put a sale sign on it, your product would sell fast. Later, you found out most of your products, if not all of them, are still stored in a warehouse or fulfillment center across the country. Meanwhile, you are spending money on storage fees, website hosting, and maybe advertising with little or no result.

This book will guide you through different ideas and marketplaces where you can generate money the same day. There are different methods of selling your product, which will vary by marketplace. Set your prices accordingly, while your product might sell well on Amazon for $35; it does not mean it will be successful on eBay for the same price.

Time value of money states a dollar today, is worth more than a dollar in the future because the dollar today, can be invested to generate interest or additional revenue. All being equal, it is best for you to sell your inventory as quickly as possible, especially if it has an expiration date. In addition, you must account for warehousing fees and any other expenses related to keeping your inventory unsold. You have to adjust your price, so your product sells quickly, but not too quickly. If your product sells too fast, it could mean your price is too low.

Before we jump into sales, we must make sure your product and marketing materials are ready for prime time. That way, we convert as many visitors as possible into paying customers. It is recommended you read this book page by page and analyze its content. Put into practice what you learn along the way. Selling is not an easy journey, but together we can make the necessary improvements to make your product more appealing to your customers.

This book is full of amazing resources to help you accomplish your task. Two important websites where you can get a lot of work completed for you include Fiverr and UpWork. Save those links and visit those websites often. Also, it will be a good idea to mention other popular websites where you can get freelancers to help you with specific task. Logo design, virtual assistant, you name it; you will find the help you need in one of the following websites: Freelancer.com, Guru, We Work Remotely, Folyo.me, Hirable, Onsite.io, Envato Studio, and Krop.com.

Never fear, there are many ways to place your product in front of consumers. With more technology becoming available and more people getting connected to the Internet, and especially social media, it is easier to get in front of the right audience. Not cheap, but easier.

There are many ways to cut costs by avoiding expensive advertising that in many cases, will not generate the expected result. For every dollar invested, you must get a return of at least one dollar in revenue and additional value like new customers or new emails you can target in the future to generate additional revenue. In this book I shall put you through some moves/steps on how to sell like no one...enjoy reading!!

A GOOD PHOTO SELLS, BUT A GREAT PHOTO SELLS MORE

Product images are important, because the images present the functions and features of the product that can also be accompanied by descriptions. Some products are easier than others to photograph. To build trust, you have to make your store look professional and ready to backup your product at all times. It's not just a good webpage design that attracts customers, you also need excellent images and recommendations from previous customers.

Taking photos of your product is easier than a video and costs less. There are different ways to go about it. If you do not know about photography, you can search on Yelp.com or online for local product photographers. Remembers that most marketplaces like Amazon require images with a white background.

Smartphones are great for taking photos on the go, but not so great for product photography, because it is better to shoot with a camera with at least 20 megapixels, while most phones are below 10 megapixels. You can borrow a friend's camera or rent one. Ask a student photographer to take the photos for you or even better, send your product and pay a professional photographer to take the photos and make them store ready.

Here are some good sources to get your product photos taken:

- https://www.powproductphotography.com
- https://pixc.com
- https://www.productphotography.com
- https://viral-launch.com/photos.html
- https://www.upgradedimages.com
- http://www.industrialcolorstudios.com
- https://orbitvu.com
- https://www.bizphotographer.com
- http://pixelperfectphotography.com
- http://www.rarestudiola.com
- http://www.etherartsus.com
- http://www.snaprite.co
- https://undefeatedcreative.com
- https://nozani.com/product-photography

Products on White Photography has a simple and inexpensive rate. There is no minimum and you can email the photographer to let them know how you want the photos to be taken. Make sure you request your product be photographed at all angles possible.

THE POWER OF VIDEO

Video content is becoming popular nowadays. More and more social media and marketplaces are adapting videos on their platforms because in just a few seconds, a video can leave a lasting impression on consumers. According to Statistas, 85% of US Internet users watches online videos. According to Adobe, "Shoppers who view video are 1.81 times more likely to purchase than non-viewers."

You should have available a few videos demonstrating use of your product; and at least one video advertising the product to attract sales. If you do not have any video yet, here are some places and ideas to get you started:

Rent a Camera. - You can rent a camera and shoot your own video. A few places where you can rent a camera include Rent-A-Center, Samy's Camera, ShareGrid, Ver, Lens Rentals, and Borrow Lenses.

Get a Videographer.- Use your local listing to find a professional video company that can help you in getting a video for your product. It depends on your budget and what are you looking for. You can also find help at your local university with students in media courses.

Some service providers will travel to you or will require you bring your product to their studio or ship the product to them. Here are some online vendors to get you started: LocalEyes, SmartShoot, Video Review Labs, Kyro Digital, LemonLight, Epipheo, blueforest studios, and Demo This.

Do It Yourself Video: You can use Microsoft Powerpoint to create slides and presentations about your product, then convert those slides into a video you can upload to YouTube. The following tools let you put together video footages and photos into their templates you can use to create your own video.

You can use your cell phone to create some footage and combine it with royalty free images and other video footage. YouTube, Reevio, Biteable, Magistro, Autodemo, Promoshin, Smilebox, Videomaker, Animakr, Kizoa, RawShorts, Style.io, Animoto, GoAnimate, Moovly, Shakr, and Movavi.

You can also use *Canva.com* and Piktochart.com to give life to your video. If you use your smartphone for photos, you can use software or apps to enhance those photos. A simple and free app is call **FocusEffect** (IOS, Android), which allows you to blur the background to make your photo look more professional.

INCLUDE POWERFUL WORDS TO INCREASE SALES

Words make a big different when selling your product. You have to include these words in the title, descriptions, and bullet points. We can start by working on the title of your product. Not the name, but titles you can use on websites, email lists, eBooks, blogs articles, press releases, etc.

Sharethrough - Create engaging headlines.

Title-Generator.com - Write a keyword to get a list of titles.

Portent - Title generator.

Once you get your title, work on your description by including powerful words that create confidence and emotion. Some powerful words and how you can use them are "**and** instead of but," because "**and**" gives the sense there is more included in the deal, while "but" gives a negative feeling. Use the word "**because**" which provides an explanation of the why and is a way to answer predetermined questions from customers.

Use "**or**" to show your customers they have more than one option. The word "**you**" creates a connection between the seller and the buyer because the buyer will feel the information is speaking directly to them. Use the word "**do**" instead of "try" because "do" is more committed and has the greatest confidence tone.

In your bullet points and your product description, highlight the benefits of your product and not the features, because ***customers are more interested in knowing what the product can do for them**** than reading a plain description of your product.

Example of features: Buy this backpack because it has YKK zipper, ripstop fabric, large capacity, and many compartments.

Example of benefits: Buy this backpack because it comes with zippers that will protect your content from sharp objects like screwdrivers, pens, and other sharp objects. It keeps your content secured. The fabric provides protection against tearing and ripping, which are one of the main causes of backpack failures. Its large capacity allows you to store more items than a regular backpack.

What description do you think will sell the product better? Exactly, the one that highlights benefits, because benefits sell.

SELLING YOUR PRODUCT ON AMAZON

Amazon is one of the highly popular online marketplaces where entrepreneurs gather and establish their businesses on. While Amazon offers a lucrative business opportunity, it pays to know and apply some guidelines that will make selling products on Amazon more successfull.

Read Amazon's Guidelines

If there is anything most important for you to do to become a fine seller on Amazon, it is no other than to learn and be familiar with the guidelines set by this website on making money. Simply browse through the site and look for the page where commonly asked questions are answered. You can also look on the announcement board for sellers where you can read about details on technical issues or performance of the site.

List Items/Manage Inventory

Item listing is also another aspect of Amazon selling you need to learn. Likewise, there is a dedicated page on the site where steps and rules for listing items can be read. Inventory must be updated on a daily basis, particularly when you are also selling the same products on other sites. Set the price for your items by first checking out how many other sellers sell products similar to yours. When it comes to pricing, do not be so attached to the actual price of your product. You can sell quickly and easily on Amazon by first checking out what the lowest offered price by other sellers for that item is. Then, price your item one percent less than this.

Manage Orders

Instead of relying only on notifications via e-mail, it will do well for you if you will check your seller account regularly. Provide your customers with timely handling of returns and refunds. Refund of orders should be done within 48 hours; refund issues must be completed within five business days upon receipt of orders. Good customer service also involves promptly answering client e-mails in 24 hours.

Complete Your Selling Tasks

Two days after you have been notified of the order, the items must already be dispatched. The item must include a packing slip. Always include your address in case the package needs to be returned. Include a note encouraging the customer to send you a feedback using the contact information you have provided. Follow Amazon's guidelines on delivery.

Provide Professional Customer Service

Inquiries from buyers via e-mail must be responded to in 24 hours. This will help promote good feedback from them and a good buyer-seller relationship with them. Remember to always use the specified language for answering queries.

Answer customer queries tactfully and clearly. If the client asked for the condition of your product, you should always tell them honest answers like stating the exact condition of the product, including tears and other possible flaws.

Protect Your Security

Regular changing of your password is necessary to make your seller account safe from hackers. You should also consider having a separate financial account especially for accepting disbursements from Amazon. Always remember that Amazon will not require disclosure of personal and financial information via e-mail. It is best to type the address of the website on the browser bar rather than clicking provided links in the e-mail.

HOW TO BOOST SALES ON AMAZON

Amazon is widely recognized as the most powerful online retail portal in the e-commerce market. On Amazon, you can discover a huge number of different sellers, millions of quality products, and a wonderful earning opportunity. Some sellers do not know the most

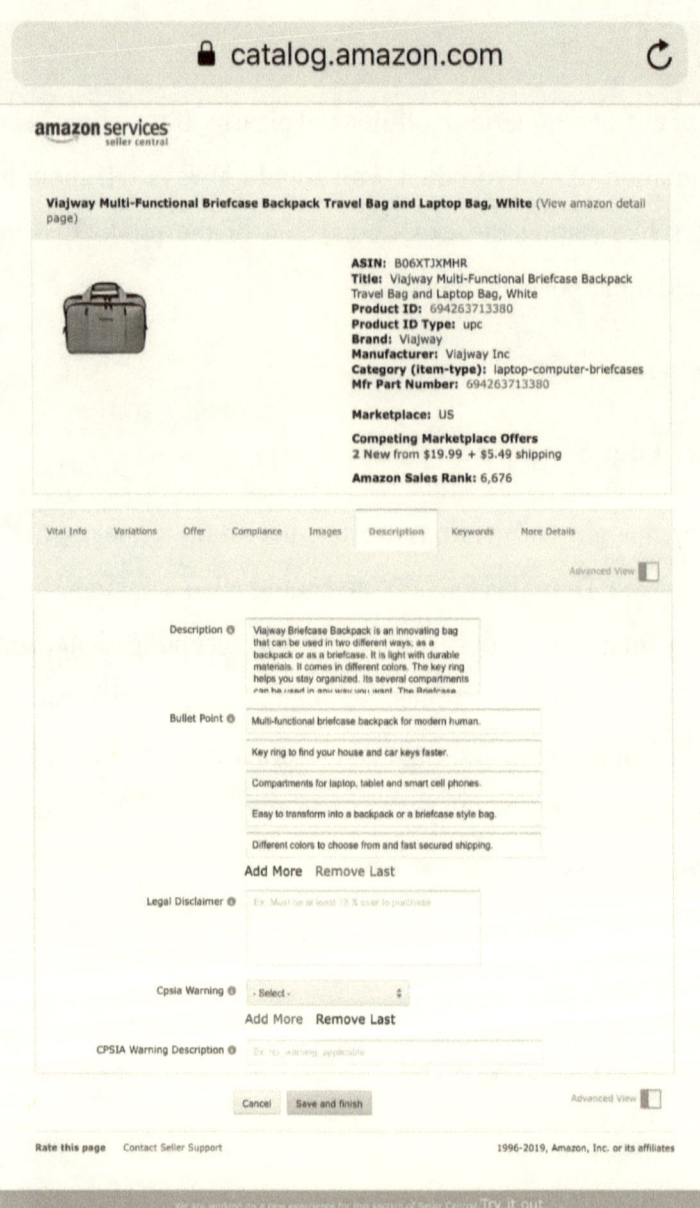

resourceful ways on how to rank at a higher position on Amazon. You can boost your sales on Amazon, only if you apply the most excellent ways in terms of Amazon SEO tactics to sell your products.

When you start selling on Amazon, it is essential to have an adequate quantity of products in your listing. Evidently, the consumers will like your products and you can get a hold of more orders. You should attempt to sell your products on Amazon at reasonable rates. In this aspect, you should change your prices frequently and check what your competitors are offering at what prices? This is the most excellent way to hold onto more customers. Another advantage is if there is a bigger demand for your products, you can to some extent increase your price and get more earnings.

Quality Product Images

Pictures are very important for driving transformations, as buyers need to figure out what they are purchasing. The entire product image must be visible and should take up approximately 80% of the space. The images should not incorporate watermarks, borders, animation, and seller logos.

Bullet Points Product Description

On Amazon, different customers seem to be searching for your product with a different need. Hence, the shorter you are in your descriptions, the more obliging you are to the customers to choose your product. Excess of information also leads your customer going away from your page, and hence, the product description should be kept under 200 words, and as per Amazon's guidelines.

Most product categories will also allow up to five bullet points. There should be more advanced details you would like to include, so limit bullet points to features with the wide-ranging appeal.

Amazon sponsored products

If you are looking to expose your product in front of as many people as possible, go for Amazon sponsored products. This facilitates your product to be displayed below search results, and in the right-hand feature or on product detail pages.

Improve your Amazon SEO

In addition to seller's rating and price, Amazon also glances at the keywords in the product's title in order to rank listings. Within the product title, you should incorporate as many keywords as possible to make sure your product is visible to the maximum audience. Amazon recommends including brand name, product description, material, size, color and number in this field. You are permitted to make use of five keywords to be entered at this juncture, so use them intelligently.

Advertising

If you are just starting out or looking to your product in front of as many eyeballs as possible, try Amazon sponsored products. This enables your product to be displayed below search results, in the right-hand column or on detail pages. If you are very familiar about marketing and advertising, do not just waste money on Amazon advertising. Advertise on Facebook, it can produce better results.

Marketing outside of Amazon

Even though email communications and direct calls belong to an old school of thought and that can lead people away from your Amazon

Store. This doesn't mean you can't market to people. You can write articles and blogs to achieve this target, you can target your relevant class with relevant content for free via Word Press. There are lots of sites which let you invite your customers by writing articles for free.

Discounts

Discounts play an important role in diverting sales graphs to a high level and building a bond between seller and buyers. Daily deals and significant discounts could land you at #1 for your product category. This also opens up the possibility of appearing on the Amazon home page under the "Hot Deals" and "New & Noteworthy" categories, which will generate enormous amounts of traffic.

Amazon seller central: Fulfillment by Amazon (FBA)

Amazon allows sellers to use its logistics network to store and deliver their products. Amazon stores your products in its warehouse, then packs and ships them, as well as providing the after sales care.

Products that are offered through FBA can be sold to members of Amazon's Prime loyalty scheme. Prime customers represent an estimated 6% of buyers, but they buy as much as 17% of total sales.

Adding your products on Vendor Express was quick and easy. Vendor Express is now closed.

1. Log into your Seller Central account at https://sellercentral.amazon.com/

2. Add your products by clicking on the Products Tab

3. Enter your product information

4. Enter the relevant product attributes

5. Choose your preferred shipping method and fill out the pricing details.

INCREASING YOUR CONVERSION RATE ON AMAZON

A good conversion rate on Amazon can help increase your sales. Now, the question arises of how can you increase your conversion rate on Amazon? First of all, you should make sure your listing is accurately optimized. Only then can you convert most of the traffic that Amazon directs to your listing. A good conversion rate on Amazon can be increased by considering the following factors: -

1. 'Title' is one of the most significant elements of your product listing on Amazon. A majority of the buyers review products by the title, in view of the fact it explains about your product. Amazon has recommended strict guidelines, and wants your title to be short, descriptive and most relevant. Thus, you are required to incorporate the most appropriate keywords in the title. It will help your product's rank get higher, and increase your conversion rate on Amazon.

2. The main image for your product that you are selling should be of superior quality and eye-catching. Amazon wants the conversion of the visitors who are clicking on the different products available on their website. The high-quality product images serve as an influential factor in determining the conversion rate.

3. There can be some customers who may be unimpressed by your product title or the images. But still, you can set out for the bullets point description, as recommended by Amazon. Amazon's bullet points are moderately clear-cut, and utilizing them can help you achieve a good rare of conversion.

4. Another most important factor for getting an excellent conversion rate and an increase in sales is the customers' review section. The reviews posted by customers have a great impact on your listing on Amazon. This will further decide your conversion rate, in addition to the product sales.

Amazon has its own search engine, and their main target is to sell high-quality products and earn maximum profits. They evaluate the product's ranking by calculating the inflow of traffic and the conversion rate. The product listing should incorporate the most appropriate keywords that are to be optimized. Hence, you're required to provide the product listing in Amazon's prearranged format.

INCREASE SALES AND CONVERSION RATES WITH ZEN CART

Your conversion rate will tell you how many visitors are taking a certain action - it could be completing a purchase (obviously, the ultimate goal) but could also include completing a contact form, signing up for a newsletter, etc. You can measure this by setting up goals within your analytics program. This will give you valuable statistics and metrics which you can use to measure against and help improve your business.

You need to optimize the functionality of the cart. The more clicks you make a visitor perform in order to get to the end result, the more likely they are to leave without doing anything. "Abandoning the process" is a big problem in Ecommerce.

Below are ways you can optimize and improve the cart and shopping experience for the customer:

- **Simplify the login / registration page**
  - Rephrase blocks of text to make the user think less
  - Remove unnecessary information at signup (DOB, phone, etc)

- Reduce the amount of clicks necessary to signup, increase white space and create a better flow to the process

- **Remove the create an account success screen**

Just adds another click. After signup, take the user directly to the next screen they were expecting to visit.

- Make the Add to Cart, View Cart, Checkout, Continue and Submit Order buttons/links more visible, prominent and compelling

Self explanatory. You want to make sure these important buttons stand out from the rest of the website. It will draw the users' attention and make them subconsciously follow the process you want them to

- Clearly indicate an item has been added to the cart, and don't send them to their cart after adding an item

By default the user will be taken to their cart when they add a product. You want to skip this and let them continue to shop and add more products

- **Simplify the shopping cart page**

Remove unnecessary text, such as "Visitor carts being merged with member carts," etc. Just confuses people. Remove the estimate shipping button and add that section directly on the page, it reduces clicks and confusion

- **Make changes to the checkout shipping page**

    o Change the language
    o Add white space
    o Display the checkout button prominently

- **Make changes to the checkout payment page**

    o Same steps as mentioned above with checkout shipping page

- **Reword the checkout confirmation page**

Change the language so the user is not confused. Make sure they're aware that one more step is necessary to complete the transaction

Add the word "Edit" to the images

Modify the layout of the credit card information screen

- **Optimize the thank you page**

The one time that you have the user's utmost attention is on the "thank you" page. It is one page people not only read, but read carefully and take note of. Why? Because they want to find out what the next steps are for receiving the product they just ordered.

With the above information at hand, this is the page we should ask them to refer friends and add incentives - Receive a discount if you refer a friend, etc.

You could also provide a customer service survey at this page as well, so you can collect data that will help you to continually improve your cart

- **Create an impulse offer - FREE SHIPPING**

Studies have shown time and time again that free shipping promotions are powerful offers which almost always result in an increase in sales

- **Simplify navigation where possible**

Where possible you should reduce the amount of clicks it takes to find what the user is looking for.

- **Build customer confidence**

Prominently display secure and SSL images/certifications, return policies, phone numbers, etc.

- **Add as many payment methods as possible**

CyberSource reported retailers who offered three or more payment options saw an average of 14% increase in conversions. And Forrester Research contends that alternative payment methods help increase sales and reduce shopping cart abandonment

The following modules/add-ons is recommended:

- **Amazon Inventory Loader**

This will allow you to export the products into an Amazon account where we can list and sell products

- **Best Sellers Page**

This creates a page that will list best selling items

- **Contest System**

By installing this, you can add a contest signup side box and offer the customer the chance to win something in exchange for their email address, which you then load into your email marketing program

- **Google Froogle Feed**

Same functionality as the Amazon Inventory Loader, this adds the products to Froogle for sale

- **Better Together**

Allows crossselling at a discount; a product can be linked with another specific product, another product from a specific category, or any other product, with an associated discount (in dollars or % off) if both are purchased together

- **Order Steps**

Creates a graphic indicator of where you are in the checkout process

- **Free Shipping Rules**

This shipping module allows you to offer free shipping when more than one requirement is set. These requirements include order total, total weight, and total items. For example, if the minimum order total is set to $1,000 and the maximum weight is set to 5lbs, free shipping would only be given for orders that meet BOTH of these requirements

- **Tell a Friend - Free Shipping**

This module will give the customer free or reduced shipping if they tell a friend using the form on the website.

INCREASE YOUR SALES USING THIS SHOPPING CART TIP

Learn how to upsell using this shopping cart tip, and dramatically increase your sales. Everyone has heard the saying, "Would you like fries with that?"

It's called an **upsell, a "sales technique whereby (one) attempts to have the customer purchase more expensive items, upgrades, or other add-ons** in an attempt to make a more profitable sale." (Wikipedia.com).

Recently I was offered a brilliant upsell. We were at the mall, ordering lunch and a lemonade, when the clerk asked me this:

"Would you like a large drink instead? It's 50 cents more and twice the size!"

Wow, I thought, that's a good upsell! So I asked her, "How many people go for this?"

She told me 75% of people take the upsell at the point of ordering and get the large size. She went on to say they raised the price of the small drink just so they could say that phrase to the customer. The regular used to be $1.75 compared to the large, which was $3.00. Pretty clever, huh?

But upsells don't belong only to the fast food industry. This tactic can be highly profitable to an Internet business. Amazon.com, for example, is a master at it. Have you noticed that, when you order a book at Amazon, their website always suggests another, similar book that you might want to add to your purchase?

If you are like most of my clients, you would love to configure your shopping cart so it can handle this profitable strategy.

There are many different ways to upsell to your customers. You need to take into account your business, your products, your market, and your level of aggression, since some techniques are more pushy than others.

Amazon sellers' URLs:

• Seller Central: https://sellercentral.amazon.com

- Fulfillment by Amazon: https://services.amazon.com/fulfillment-by-amazon/benefits.htm

- Vendor Express: https://vendorexpress.amazon.com/ CLOSED

One great tool to use with Amazon is called Kibly. Kibly is the only tool approved by Amazon to send emails to customers automatically. As you might know, the customers belong to Amazon, and Amazon will not share customers emails with vendors. Amazon has an email tool to send email to customers, but you can not send mass emails automatically. Kibly, is useful for the main concept is to obtain as many positive product reviews as possible.

Kibly: https://kibly.com

SELLING ON EBAY

Ebay is one of the largest online marketplaces. It gives the seller options to list their products as an auction or a fixed price. It also has a classified website that functions as a marketplace, but with the idea of focusing on local consumers.

Recently, eBay announced splitting with Paypal and adding Adyen as its main provider. Ebay acquired Paypal a few years back, but Carl Icahn pushed to separate Paypal from eBay. After the spinoff, Carl Icahn opted for Paypal instead of eBay. According to Engadget.com, eBay and Paypal have a payment agreement until 2023.

More payment options are good for sellers, because some customers have different preference when paying. Ebay has not announced any payment structure for the future as yet. As of today, eBay is still one of the best merchants to get money the same day. If you sell your product on eBay and you are using Paypal as your payment method, you get the payment in your account, the same day. This option is not available with Amazon, Walmart, Groupon, or any other major marketplace.

One good feature for buyers, is when buyers can search items by distance. Buyers can search, for example, an item no more than 100 miles from their zip code. Even with that feature available, there are many items sold by vendors in different countries. Buyers have to wait 30 to 45 days to get their items. If you live in a popular area in United States, you can advertise or write on your description that the item will be received no later than 7 days. Most consumers would rather pay a bit more to get their items faster than having to wait more than 30 days for their purchase.

Ebay buyers love free shipping. Account for shipping cost by including it in the item price. Like previously mentioned, other vendors from different countries like China are also selling on eBay. Some of those vendors are selling items highly discounted and you have to compete on pricing. Search the product that you are selling on eBay and if you do not find it, use a similar item as reference. Once you find several vendors selling the same or similar items, analyse the prices, locations, seller ratings, and quality of the product.

You can buy discounted shipping labels on eBay. Amazon is the provider that gives sellers the largest shipping discount through UPS. Another company is Shopify, which I noticed my discount was bigger after selling and shipping many items with Shopify. Even though Shopify is younger than eBay, you get better shipping rates with Shopify.

Some important eBay links for sellers:

eBay fees calculator: https://www.fees.ebay.com/feeweb/feecalculator

eBay Seller Central: https://pages.ebay.com/seller-center/index.html

eBay opens your store: https://pages.ebay.com/seller-center/run-your-store/set-up-your-store.html

SMARTPHONE APPS THAT SELL

To be honest, placing your product everywhere takes time and patience. You must keep the information and prices updated on every site because you do not want a big discrepancy in pricing from one site to the other. Placing your product in more websites and marketplaces does not guarantee more sales, but it could help your sales and number of visitors. You can later revisit and analyze if the time and resources, to place your product on certain websites, are worth spending. If it's not worth it, you can just focus on those giving you better results.

I recommend three particular apps for these companies to spend money advertising online, radio and on television. They have many subscribers and available items for sale which creates additional opportunities to increase sales in your local area and save in shipping. Since you do not have packing and shipping expenses, you can pass on these savings to local customers by reducing the price accordingly.

LetGo

This app has become one of the top selling app marketplaces for used goods in local areas. It advertises on local television and cable networks, which helps in creating a large community of local buyers and sellers. It is one of the fastest growing app with over 75 million downloads and more than 200 million listings.

LetGo includes many categories where you can place your listing. It is free to post a listing and you will be dealing locally. I recommend if you sell a product you can keep in your car for hours or days, to always carry some with you at all times because you do not know when a sale happens and it is good to be prepared to close the deal as soon as possible. Visit their website and download the app today https://letgo.com or from your phone App Store or Google Play, search for LetGo to download the app.

OfferUp

OfferUp is another popular community selling app. You can easily find and buy cars, clothing, furnitures, entertainment, games, movies, and services in your area. It is free to buy and sell and posting to this app will increase your chances of getting additional customers. If you post a listing and it's being over 3 weeks and people are not showing interest for your listing; revise the title, description, and price and repost.

Sometimes, it requires a little push from you by being available to answer prospective customer's questions as soon as possible. Smartphone app shoppers usually ask several questions before buying the product. They will lose interest if the questions are not answered quickly. Also, remember that when a customer shows some interest in your product, the customer is also looking for alternatives before making the final decision.

If you want to close the deal, you have to jump ahead of your competition. Who says you cannot contact visitors that favored your product? Go ahead and contact them and try to close the deal. Visit their website and download the app today https://offerup.com/ or from your phone at the App Store or Google Play, search for OfferUp to download the app.

5 Miles

Lately, 5 Miles had changed its design and had implemented new features like the option of paying through the app and selling outside your local area by charging customers for delivery. I recommend you stay local and focus and selling consumers around your areas for a better price. Let your community knows you are open for business and that you love their support.

The app also provides you with a custom URL you can use to promote your product. The link creates a store with all your products listed. If you want a store and you do not want to spend money on hosting and domain, this is a good way to start.

5 Miles started advertising heavily late 2015, but the app is more focused on adding more features now. Visit their website and download the app today https://5miles.com or from your phone at the App Store or Google Play, search for 5 Miles to download the app.

Groupon

Groupon has Store and Merchant account services to help you sell your products. Placing your products on Groupon expands your business to a lot more customers looking for good products with nice discounts. Shipping and handling and customer service is handled by you. You do not have access to customer's emails, but you can communicate with them by opening a ticket when they order your products.

Groupon takes 15% commission of the total amount collected, including shipping. Their payment schedule is by the 10th and 25th of every month. For example, orders marked as delivered from the 1st - 15th of the month are paid by the 25th of the month. Orders marked as delivered from the 16th - 31st of the month are paid the 10th of the following month. If you had $275 in sales and collected $25 in shipping your grand total is equal to $300 minus 15% Groupon's fees ($45) your net pay out is $255.

One of the best things about Groupon, their fees are plain and simple comparatively with Amazon complicated when using Fulfill by Amazon (FBA). Groupon used to charge 15% only on the sales portion and not shipping collected, but recently, they changed their policy and started charging the 15% on the grand total. It seems unfair, considering that most sellers actually lose money with shipping. For that reason, if you provide free shipping or low rate shipping, you have to find a way to include it in the product price or it will end up costing you too much. Small and light products are easy and inexpensive to ship, but large and heavy items like luggage and rolling backpacks, cost too much to ship.

The idea is not just selling, but selling and making a profit. It's not complicated to get approved on Groupon. You can start selling your products in no time. Of course, they can take a few days to approve your product. In the meantime, have your products ready for shipping. Depending of the popularity of your product, you can easily can get 6 or more orders per day. You have to make sure that you are placing your product price on Groupon, at least 5% below the market price (Amazon, Walmart, Target, etc) to be place into the Flash Deal. Groupon buyers are constantly looking for best deals online. Make sure your price is competitive without losing money.

Once your product starts selling, make sure you answer questions to customers fast and try shipping within 24 hours to keep your account in good health, which increases the chances of your products getting more views on Groupon. Always keep your products that look they are more than 20% OFF to reach the Flash Deal page and attract more sales. Search for similar products and see what they are doing and how they are doing it. Are you competing for better quality, lower price, or both?

Groupon Merchant: https://www.groupon.com/merchant/join

Wish.com

Wish.com is a large marketplace like no other. The characteristics of Wish is that it sells highly discounted items from international vendors. You might not complete in price, but do you want to wait 30 or 45 days to get an item? They might even forget what they purchased. By promoting yourself as a local vendor and delivering quickly to your customers, it creates an opportunity for you to increase sales in your niche.

When you submit your product, your product will be visible on Wish.com and the Wish app. Wish reaches around 300 million consumers in Europe and United States. You can concentrate mostly in one market if you are not familiar with international shipping and how much it will cost you to ship the product overseas.

Most products on Wish required shipping payment. If you are selling your product with free shipping on one site, you can reduce the product price on Wish and account for shipping collected. Wish might take around 15% of your sale and this is called Revenue Shared. The Revenue Shared percentage is based on what you are selling. Wish does not have a flat rate like Groupon has.

Another thing to take into consideration is Wish imposes up to 20% penalty to Merchants that deliver item past the five business days. It might suspend your account too. Wish has options to boost your products by paying some advertising fees.

Here are some important Wish links:

Merchant registration: https://merchant.wish.com

Merchant policy: https://merchant.wish.com/policy/home

Merchant mobile apps: https://merchant.wish.com/mobile

Merchant signup guide: https://merchantfaq.wish.com/hc/en-us/articles/219188967

Brand University: https://merchant.wish.com/brand-university

Let your body relax and make other people do all the hard selling work for you

Have you ever heard about affiliate programs? Yes, it is a powerful tool that can be used to generate additional sales. Some affiliate companies get better success promoting some products than others; some of them concentrate on specific product, for example, digital products. *The best advocates about your products are your customers, they can easily create a virtual selling force that can generate additional sales across social networks.*

All you have to provide them is the tools for easily sharing information and images about your products and an easy way to share information with their friends and family in social medias like Twitter, Instagram, Facebook, Pinterest, Tumblr, and others. To incentivize their participation, you can offer some type of discount or create a loyalty program where they earn points, money, rebates, or prizes for sharing purchases on their social network.

There are different major websites that can help you get thousands of affiliates associates in just of few days or hours. Some of these companies might require up front payment to cover the cost of sales, clicks, or leads generated by their affiliates. You decide how much to spend. If you have an advertising budget, even better, because you can allocate some of that money according to where you get best results. It would not make sense having affiliate associates if you only have a few units in inventory. Even large companies like Walmart, that generate billions in sales, use affiliate programs to increase sales and attract new customers.

Here is a list of top companies where you can find affiliates to advertise your product:

- Amazon
- MyPoints
- Rakuten Marketing
- CJ
- ShareASale
- MaxBounty
- ClickBank
- Pepperjam
- FlexOffers
- AvantLink
- RevenueWire

The list below is for mobile apps that reward shoppers for certain actions like visiting your store or purchasing your product:

- ShopKick
- Ibotta
- Key Ring
- Make Money
- EasyShift
- SlideJoy
- Perk

Find updated list at https://TuOpinion.org.

INTRODUCTION TO DROP SHIPPING

What is drop shipping and how does it work? Is it really a valid supply chain management model? Can anyone take advantage of this technique? The truth is that drop shipping is actually a very simple process and a low cost entry point to buying and selling online.

The drop shipping business model works as follows: a retailer finds a product from a company that is willing to drop ship, and then lists that product on an online auction or an eCommerce website. The retailer, then, is in charge of the promotion of that product and collecting the payment for it, but they are never actually in possession of the item.

THE CLEAR ADVANTAGES OF DROP SHIPPING

If you are a large firm, promoting a specific type of items, it may be to your advantage to purchase wholesale. The clear benefit is that by purchasing in large quantities, your wholesaler will consent to sell you the products at quite a low unit cost, which provides you with the opportunity for a greater price mark-up.

However, the wholesaler, to be able to do this, will ordinarily require you to purchase products in large quantities and will typically decline to re-purchase anything you can't get rid of. That is why the unit price is as low as it is. If you are a huge company and you recognize you have a steady demand for the product you are offering, it is more than likely worth the risk to get into wholesale buying.

Alternatively, if you are an Amazon, eBay vendor or a smaller Internet dealer, you can't afford to assume the risks of purchasing at wholesale. Where would you warehouse all the unsold merchandise? How would you deal with returns? How will you package and ship and what will that end up costing you?

Drop shipping solves all of these difficulties for a price. The price is that you will shell out greater than a wholesale cost for the products you are vending. The benefit of drop shipping is you are not required to pay for an item before you sell it, so storing of unsold items need not be considered. This means you will never need to agonize about being stuck with unsold products that are no longer popular when a newer and better product arrives on the market.

When you make use of drop shipping, you will have the choice to promote lots of diverse types of items from a number of suppliers and so you are able to always promote what's hot right now. Your drop shipping company will package and ship the products you have ordered immediately on payment. You will have already received the retail price you are charging your customer and therefore you will always have the cash to pay your drop shipper.

Most, but not all, drop shipping companies will agree to put your name or your firm's name on the package, but the return address will always be that of the drop shipping company because that's where returns will be sent to. If the item is broken or damaged, the drop shipper will, as a rule, replace it and ship the replacement to the customer. If the item is returned only because the buyer didn't care for it and returned it, the drop shipping company will refund you the money they charged you less their costs incurred in getting the product to your buyer. You should be especially watchful to make sure you totally comprehend and consent to the re-stocking and other terms of your drop shipper before you do any business with them.

HOW CAN BUSINESS OWNERS OFFER DROP SHIPPING TO INCREASE SALES

Drop shipping is an extremely popular business model for new business owners, especially Gen Zers and Millennials, due to Internet marketing skills far outweighing financial capacity. Since you don't need to stock or handle the items you are selling, it's possible to start a drop shipping business with limited funds.

An e-commerce website that operates a drop shipping model purchases the items it sells from a third-party supplier or manufacturer, who then fulfills the order. This not only cuts operational costs, but it also frees up your time to focus all of your efforts on customer acquisition.

If you are ready to start a business that can compete with retail giants, and do so on a limited budget, then follow these steps below to increase in sales. While it doesn't take a lot of startup funds to launch a drop shipping business, it will require an immense amount of hard work.

1. Select a niche

The niche you select needs to be laser-focused and something you are genuinely interested in. A product range that isn't focused will be difficult to market. If you aren't passionate about the niche you select, you will be more apt to becoming discouraged, because it takes a lot of work to successfully scale a drop shipping business. Here are some points to consider when selecting your niche:

Seek attractive profits. When you are running a drop shipping business model, your focus is on marketing and customer acquisition, so the amount of work required to sell a $20 item is essentially the same as it would be to sell a $1,500 item. Select a niche with higher-priced products.

Low shipping costs are very important. Even though your supplier or manufacturer will handle the shipping, if the cost is too high, it will act as a customer repellant. Find something that is inexpensive to ship, as this also gives you the option of offering free shipping to your customers and absorbing that cost as a business expense in order to attract more sales.

Make sure your product appeals to impulse buyers with disposable income. When you are focused on driving traffic to your website, you want to experience the highest conversion rate possible because most visitors will never return. The products you are selling should trigger impulse buys and appeal to those with the financial ability to make a purchase on the spot.

Make sure people are actively searching for your product. Use Google's Keyword Planner and Trends to check some common search terms related to your potential niche. If nobody is searching for what you are planning on selling, you are dead in the water before you even begin.

Create your own brand. Your drop shipping business will have more value if you can rebrand whatever it is you are selling and pass it off as your own. Look for a product or line you can white label and sell as your own brand with custom packaging and branding.

Sell something that isn't readily available locally. Pick something your customer can't find down the street. That way, you become more attractive to a potential customer.

2. Perform competition research

Remember, you will you be competing with other drop shipping operations, as well as retail giants like Walmart and Amazon. This is where a lot of potential drop shippers go wrong, because they look for a product that has little to no competition. That's a sign there isn't demand for that particular product.

There are many reasons why a product might not have a lot of competition, like high shipping costs, supplier and manufacturing issues or poor profit margins. Look for products that have competition, as it's a sign that there is a high demand and the business model is sustainable.

3. Secure a supplier

Partnering with the wrong supplier can ruin your business, so it's important you don't rush this step. Conduct proper due diligence. Most drop shipping suppliers are located overseas, making communication extremely important, both in terms of response speed and the ability to understand each other. If you are not 100 percent confident in the communication abilities of a potential supplier, move on and continue your search.

Try to learn from other entrepreneurs who have walked this path in the past. There are plenty of information sources available, from business and tech blogs to this subreddit about drop shipping. It's a popular topic that can help you avoid costly supplier mistakes.

4. Build your e-commerce website

The fastest way to launch a website that supports a drop shipping business model is to use a simple e-commerce platform like Shopify. You don't need a tech background to get up and running, and it has plenty of apps to help increase sales.

Even if you have a sizeable budget that would allow you to hire a web design and development company to create a custom solution, it's a much wiser move to use one of the plug-and-play options, especially in the beginning. Once you are established and the revenue is coming in, then you can explore additional website customization.

5. Create a customer acquisition plan

Having a great product and a website is great, but without customers looking to buy, you don't have a business. There are several ways to attract potential customers, but the most effective option is to start a Facebook ad campaign.

This allows you to generate sales and revenue right from the start, which can contribute to quick scaling. Facebook allows you to place your offer directly in front of a highly targeted audience. This gives you the ability to compete with the largest brands and retailers immediately.

You also have to think long-term, so search engine optimization and email marketing should also be a focus. Collect emails from the start and setup automated email sequences offering discounts and special offers. It's an easy way to leverage your existing customer base and generate revenue without additional advertising and marketing spend.

6. Analyze and optimize

You need to track all of the data and metrics available to grow your business. This includes Google Analytics traffic and Facebook conversion pixel data, if that is your main customer acquisition channel. When you are able to track every single conversion -- to know where the customer originated from and what path they took on your website that eventually led to a sale -- it enables you to scale what works and eliminate what doesn't.

You will never have a set-and-forget advertising or marketing solution. You need to constantly test new opportunities and fine-tune current campaigns, which allows you to know when to optimize or shift campaign spending.

BENEFITS OF DROP SHIPPING

The benefits of drop shipping are many and varied and no other process involves such a great prospect of profits. Drop shipping has become a really popular business. Millions of people are already involved in this business and several millions more look forward to joining it. What is it that makes this business so popular? What are the various benefits associated with this process? This book will help you to understand the various advantages that drop shipping offers and how we can use it to boost our sales.

Basically, drop shipping involves a person who acts as a middleman between the wholesale seller and the customer. The order a customer places is simply passed onto the seller, who then is in charge of delivering the entire order to the customer, which also includes the shipping process. The drop shipper charges the customer a higher price and pays the wholesale seller a lower price than that offered to the customer and in this way, he makes a lot of profit.

Even, finding a wholesale seller is not difficult as we can make use of websites, which they offer a detailed listing of thousands of dealers who offer different varieties of products. Thus, the whole process is a really profitable and beneficial one.

We need not be worried about maintaining an inventory and can avoid all the costs associated with it and also not worry about where we can procure the goods and products from and the shipping process associated with the process, as the wholesale seller takes care of all these aspects.

We have to price our products in such a way we make profit out of the process. We have to remember to include shipping charges in the rate we offer to the customer, as we have to pay for this later to the wholesale seller. We also have to verify about the quality of the products offered by the wholesale seller. Thus, if we follow these tips that are mentioned, we can be sure about succeeding in this field and can make a lot of profits.

HOW TO GET YOUR PRODUCT INTO WALMART AND TARGET

If you have a product, you will come across the need to sell it to more customers. Without getting the product to leading retail stores, such as Walmart and Target, you will find it to be a difficult task to get more customers for your product. Due to this reason, you will need to have a clear understanding on how to get your product into Walmart and Target.

How to Get Your Product into Walmart

Walmart is the largest employer in the United States. Combined; its parking lots are about the size of Tampa, Florida, and its annual revenue is about $405 billion, making it the 23rd largest economy in the world. This behemoth of a company holds significant clout in the retail world, and presents a huge opportunity to anyone looking to increase volume in their product sales. So the question is: how do you get your product into Walmart?

There are a number of criteria your product needs to satisfy in order to be even considered to be put on the shelves of Walmart.

Walmart Stores, Inc. is an American public corporation that runs a chain of large discount department stores and a chain of warehouse stores. In 2010, it was the world's largest public corporation by revenue, according to the Forbes Global 2000 for that year. The company was founded by Sam Walton in 1962, incorporated on October 31, 1969, and publicly traded on the New York Stock Exchange in 1972.

Walmart, headquartered in Bentonville, Arkansas, is the largest

majority private employer and the largest grocery retailer in the United States. In 2009, it generated 51% of its US$258 billion sales

in the U.S. from grocery business. It also owns and operates the Sam's Club retail warehouses in North America.

Walmart has 8,500 stores in 15 countries, with 55 different names. The company operates under its own name in the United States, including the 50 states. It also operates under its own name in Puerto Rico. Wal-Mart operates in Mexico as Walmex, in the United Kingdom as Asda in Japan as Seiyu, and in India as Best Price. It has wholly-owned operations in Argentina, Brazil, and Canada. Wal-Mart's investments outside North America have has mixed results: its operations in the United Kingdom, South America and China are highly successful, while it was forced to pull out of Germany and South Korea when ventures there were unsuccessful.

Walmart is pretty much the biggest retailer when it comes to selling your product–but being on its shelves can create as many problems as opportunities. Here is practical advice on how to do it right.

For a small business accustomed to producing quantities in the low thousands, the opportunity to supply tens of thousands of products to 3,400 Walmart stores can be a dream come true–or a nightmare, if they are not prepared for the retailer's expectations.

Ariel Balk, founder and CEO of lingerie and swimwear brand Smart & Sexy and Nell Merlino, CEO of Count Me In, a nonprofit group that helps women entrepreneurs, are committed to helping small businesses as a path to economic growth, but in a decidedly new way–not with incremental growth, but by creating market-flexing, broad-based sales from the get-go.

On the heels of Walmart's announcement about its commitment to buy an additional $50 billion in U.S. products over the next 10 years, Balk and Merlino recently asked top $100 million sellers to Walmart to share advice with new entrepreneurs who want to prep their products for the retail giant's buyers. It's applicable to anyone who has dreamed of getting a crack at Walmart's 138 million weekly shoppers.

Experts included turn around titan Lynn Tilton, CEO of Patriarch Partners; clothing mogul Mark Adjmi, CEO of Adjmi Apparel Group; expert "closer" Joey Setton, executive vice president of Saramax Apparel Group; and licensing expert and CEO of Sequential Brands Group Yehuda Shmidman. Here's what they shared:

Your product has to fit Walmart; Walmart doesn't have to fit your product. The five panelists agree on three basics for anyone considering selling to Walmart: Does your product appeal to Walmart customers; does it fill a void on the retailer's shelves; and are you willing and able to get your costs low enough to be both profitable and meet Walmart's strict pricing strategy?

Your infrastructure has to meet order demands. Working with Walmart "is around-the-clock job, and if you are not ready for that, you should put off your effort to get on store shelves," says Balk, who ships 60 million garments out a year–many of them to Walmart. "Can you handle replenishment needs, logistics, and turn around times? If you don't have the staff to handle those things, the burden will fall on you," she says.

If you cannot hold up your end of the deal, your first chance may be your last. That's why Balk waited five years before making a deal with Walmart for her Smart & Sexy line. "I needed to understand what I needed to deliver in terms of quality and pricing and what kind of staffing was needed to meet those goals."

Shmidman says if you don't have manufacturing capabilities, you should consider licensing your product to a manufacturer as a way to scale your business to meet Walmart's volume demands. "You may be great at marketing, but if you can't make money from production, you are out of business," Shmidman says. "That's the business we're in–we may not be able to find the best factories, but we know how to build brands."

Understand the true cost of your product. It can be challenging to meet Walmart's pricing needs, which are lower than most small entrepreneurs are used to, especially if they don't know what the product actually costs to make. "People often underestimate the cost to produce their product and the overhead required to run their business," says Tilton. "It startles me so many smart people don't know the true cost of making their product. It's beyond cost of goods. Every company has to have a pricing model on every product. What is your wholesale cost? Do you have discounts? Will you take returns? What's your overhead? Do you need inspectors on the ground?" she says.

Walmart, for instance, demands that manufacturers' factories comply with their standards, and inspectors are necessary to ensure compliance. Those people cost money, which has to be worked into your bottom line.

Prepare. Once you've got an appointment with Walmart, do your homework. "Before your first one-hour meeting with a buyer, you need to put in 100 hours of research," says Adjmi. That means visiting the departments where your product will likely be stocked and really studying them–the layout, stock, traffic pattern, and shoppers in the aisle. Everything. It also means familiarizing yourself with Walmart's supplier expectations, which are detailed on its website.

"A lot of people say, 'I know my business,' but that's just half the game," Adjimi advises. "I've seen these people get blown away in Walmart meetings because they don't understand what they need to know to answer Walmart's Questions: What does the competition look like? Do your factories match Walmart's expectations? What margins are you expecting to get? Where will the product fit into the existing category mix in the stores? Is it a regional product, good for 500 stores as opposed to 2,500 stores?"

Not only do you need to know your product better than anyone, you need to know Walmart better than your competitor. "If you don't, stay home and reschedule the appointment," says Adjimi.

Be confident, yet humble. You can know everything about your product and as much as possible about Walmart's needs, but there's always that question that seems to come at you from the side. "Don't make up an answer," says Balk. "Tell them the truth–say 'I don't know but I'll get back to you tomorrow,' and then find the answer and get back to them."

Don't leave without a deal. "In order for your company to have revenue, you have to sell something," Joey Setton reminds us. That may seem like a no-brainer, but oftentimes small manufacturer's can be so overwhelmed they don't leave a buyer meeting with a purchase order in hand. "The biggest impediment to closing is not focusing on what the buyer is saying," said Setton.

He told the story of a salesman who went into Walmart with a great product displayed on a beautiful glossy easel board. Setton was excited because he really thought they had a home run. "My colleague talked about the items and price points. He was doing a great job. At one point the buyer said, 'Oh, that's a really cute item,' and she started writing notes about it. But my salesman kept going, talking about more items, flipping the easel board past that item the buyer was so intrigued with."

Setton stepped in and reengaged the buyer on the product she liked. "We spent about 45 minutes talking about how many she would take per store, even though there were 40 other products on the easel display to talk about." Ultimately, they only got through five or six pages–but they wrote orders because Setton listened to the buyer and wasn't only concerned with getting through the entire product line. "If a buyer is saying, 'Stop, I like this,' then stop–because it's likely you'll get the order. Your job is not just to try to sell; you have to close."

Below are 6 points to keep in mind that will improve your chances of getting your product into Walmart.

1. Create an innovative and quality product

All great businesses start with a unique offering in the marketplace. In order for any large retailer to do business with you, your product has to be somewhat innovative. It has to solve a problem needed by many. It also must be durable and packaged in a way so when customers buy it, it doesn't break, people can't steal it and it is designed to be seamlessly placed on Walmart's shelves. Keep this in mind as you design and develop your product and packaging. Make sure during production you adhere to Wal-Mart's requirements and build in good cost margins as Walmart will ask for pricing below wholesale.

2. Develop your brand

We are firm believers in the following statement: "Unless you stand for something, you stand for nothing." We have 10-20 of everything in the marketplace. Unless you develop your brand you risk falling into the cacophony of products only differentiating in functions and features. A well-developed brand makes your product stand heads and shoulders above the competition because of its unique story and personality.

3. Design great packaging

Package design is key. A great package design can help your product look larger than life on the shelf. A good package design dramatizes and communicates the brand to the customer while demonstrating its use, function and features. It differentiates your brand from your competitors and allows you to stand out. Our client also adds QR codes on their packaging so the customer can scan using their smart phone to see a live demonstration—which further persuades the customer to buy. This also helps you persuade the Walmart buyer when you get your 30 seconds to pitch your product.

4. Build your inventory

One thing most hunting and outdoor start-ups overlook is the ability to fulfill large orders. Walmart promises to always give customers the lowest prices on their products and they always ask for large purchase orders…always. Larger orders are typically classified as 7,000 – 10,000 units or more. If Walmart accepts your application to be a supplier, you will need to fulfill the purchase order under their terms, which could be within 15 days, and you may not get paid for 60-90 days. If you do not have a good inventory and the means to stay afloat for 3 months, this could be a deal breaker. This also relates directly to my next point about business history.

5. Build your business history and a good product case study

A lot of our past hunting and outdoor start-up clients have come to us with one thing in mind: "We want to get into Walmart, Costco, Home Depot, Sports Authority, Dick's, Lowes, Target, etc." Most haven't thought through what it takes to build their business first and are shocked when we tell them the bad news about what it entails—unless the product is truly remarkable and the client has the necessary inventory—but this is rare.

We will typically advise you to build a business case study first so when it comes time to go for it, you are equipped with a track record that says success to the Walmart sporting goods buyer. You will also learn much along the way. A simple website with online store and Internet marketing program can help you build your business and obtain valuable experience. This strategy gets the most ROI and allows you to test the validity of the product before making a significant inventory investment.

While this is taking place, we advise you to get out there and be willing to take some risks with smaller retailers. This also will provide you with much needed experience to perfect your sales pitch and allow you to test the appeal and validity of your product. Long before Walmart, our client was selling in smaller retail outlets like Sportsman Warehouse, Cabellas, Bass Pro Shops and others. This allowed them to identify and get over the many hurdles that you will face along the way.

6. Perfect your pitch and be persistent

Once you have developed your brand, designed a killer package design, built your inventory, have a deep sales history, product case study and have perfected a winning sales pitch, it's time to apply. Your presentation should be brief and to the point; it needs to showcase and demonstrate the product's value, tell the product's sales history, list customer testimonials and review and project future sales.

Once you're accepted, having other products in your product line with the same standards will allow you to expand in Walmart and potentially get into other retailers. If you get turned down, or you experience fragmented or downright rude communication, don't give up, it may take a few months or years to finally get that first meeting.

Walmart supplier application: https://corporate.walmart.com/suppliers/apply-to-be-a-supplier

Walmart Direct Import product supplier email to: gsnwpodt@walmart.com

Walmart Marketplace application: https://marketplace-apply.walmart.com/

For local suppliers, please contact your local Walmart's store manager.

HOW TO GET YOUR PRODUCT INTO TARGET

Understand your client: Before you spend a lot of time and money creating a product, you should know if anyone will want to buy it.

Learn more about Market Research

Learn if it's protectable: Know if you can defend your product against cheap copies if it gets knocked off.

Learn more about Copyright and Patent your product.

Test your product: Make sure there's a demand for your product and the customer understands what you are selling when it's on the shelf, and nobody is there to explain it.

Learn more about Product Testing

Perfect your pitch: Before you speak to decision makers, know your numbers, know your retailer and know your logistics in and out.

Learn more about pitching your product

Don't do it alone: If you haven't been successful in retail before, a secret of success is you can't do it alone. Having great sales staff, customer support and marketing partners can take you from zero to success faster than if you tried it on your own.

Learn more about retail partnerships.

By following the below mentioned steps, you will find it as an easy task to get the product you offer into Walmart.com. This is the most convenient method available to become a Walmart seller as well.

1. **Apply to become a Walmart seller**

As the first step, you should go ahead and apply to become a seller on Walmart. In order to do that, you will have to navigate to the Seller Onboarding Page. In there, you can find an "Apply Now" link. You have to click on it and fill in the required details. It will only take you around 10 minutes to complete this. That's because you will only be asked to provide your basic information such as name, email and average revenue.

2. Completing the registration

After you complete the on board form, you should go ahead and complete the registration. To do that, you will be provided with a unique link to your mailbox. You just need to follow that link and the registration process will be completed. However, you will also be asked to go through five main steps when you are completing the registration. They include adding your account details, adding partner details, adding taxes, verifying bank account and adding shipping information.

3. Complete the partner profile

As the third step, you will have to go ahead and complete the partner profile. It will provide you with access to the Seller Center. You will be able to initiate a "Checklist" in here, which can grab some of the requirements needed for launching an account. The partner profile will be the public page, where customers will be able to get more information about who you are. Hence, you should add company details, such as your company name, a short description, tax information, company policies and upload a logo. Once you complete the profile, you will be able to see how your progress bar reaches 100%. This signifies that you have successfully completed the partner profile.

4.   **Verifying your bank account**

Before you start selling, it is important to verify a bank account. To do that, you must log into the bank account, which you entered during the registration process. A penny will be credited from the bank account to verify it. This will take a couple of days to complete.

5.   **Finalizing the setup**

Now you have come to the final stage of setting up your Walmart account. You can start off by selecting the right category and right subcategory, where your product will fall into. This is a crucial step because your customers will navigate through the subcategories to locate the product. If you don't select the right subcategory, you will not be able to make enough sales.

When you are adding products, you should be extremely careful about the "Include" and "Exclude" sections. That's because the product you offer would fall into more than one category. Once you are done, you can go ahead and access the Item Setup Template. This will help you to add all the precise details about the product you offer. It is possible to configure what information out of them needs to be displayed to the guests and what information needs to be hidden. In this section, you can add an image as well. It should be a JPEG image and the maximum size should be 1MB.

6. **Test the items**

If you navigate to the Seller Center, you will be able to see an option named "Preview Item." This will assist you to verify the pricing and content, so that you can make sure everything is properly defined. You can update the inventory of your item to 1 in order to test the ordering process.

7. **Launching the account**

You are almost done with it now. All you have to do is to go ahead and launch your account, so you will be able to get customers in your way. When you are confirming the account, you will be asked to make sure all essential items are done. If you are ready to go, you should simply click on "Launch" button. This will send the request for Walmart back office team to review your profile. If there aren't any issues, your profile will be made live. This process will usually take around 24 hours to complete.

HOW TO SUBMIT PRODUCT TO TARGET

There are several ways to get a product placed in Target. However, most entrepreneurs only dream about getting their product distributed to major retailers; few actually do it. We have experienced a significant rise in interest since the show Shark Tank started airing on NBC. Mr. Checkout has had the pleasure of working with a few Shark Tank success stories such as KISStixx and 180 Party Cups, which are now being distributed around the country to stores like Walmart, Target, Kroger, 7-Eleven and more.

If you envision your product would be a good fit for Target, we have a few steps to help you get your product on their shelves.

Submit Your Product Now

We are a national distribution network of over 1,000 distributors, wagon jobbers, and merchandisers that introduce new products into stores every day with our blitz program. We are a membership organization proviing access to our database of distributors, a custom landing page on our website and access to the country's largest wholesaler network. Since 1989 we have been bringing new products to market and have seen successful placements in nearly every major big box retailer in the country. Over the years we have learned the best ways to place a product in retail stores like Target, and are available to help you accomplish your distribution goals. We make it easy:

Here are the six steps you need to take to have your product placed in Target.

1. Start with the right questions.) Before you try distributing your product to Target, you need to ask yourself a few basic questions. Do you need to build demand for your product, or is there already a demand for it? Do you know that Target would be interested in selling your product? If you can strike a deal with Target, can you handle the production volume? Do you want to sell directly to Target, or do you want to license your product to a manufacturer that will handle distribution?

2. Be prepared to profit.) Does your product offer enough of a profit margin for Target? Can you sell your product at a reasonable enough profit to cover the packaging, shipping, commissions, marketing and wholesale distribution? Check Target's guidelines for other fees you will have to build into the cost of your product for you to be able to turn enough of a profit to make an effort worth your while. If you work with a discount retailer, they will try to strip your profits down to zero to keep their prices as low as possible.

The typical breakdown of margins is: If a product costs $1 to produce, that product will retail for $4. That product that retails for $4 will wholesale for $2 to distributors and stores that purchase direct. Big box retailers like Target may offer to pay $1.25 to the manufacturer if the product costs $1 to produce. That is the typical profit margin.

3. Determine if Target is the right store for your product. The relationship between you and Target starts with you browsing their store for competing products. If Target already has a similar product, it is going to be very difficult to get your product picked up. Spend some time at your local Target to see what kind of products they are selling, speak to the manager and see if he thinks your product will sell well in their store. Picture in which zone your product would best fit on the shelf and keep in mind the most precious asset these big box stores values are their shelf space. Keep this information in mind when you are preparing your presentation to Target.

If your company is minority or women-owned, check Target's website and see if they offer specific opportunities for those designations.

4. Pitch your product to Target.) Decide whether it will be you or a representative to present your product to Target. Your presentation depends heavily on your strengths as a businessperson as they will most likely ask financial questions and logistics questions.

It's common for companies to hire a broker to pitch their product to Target, as it will be more likely your product will make it to the next stage if the individual pitching your product has industry knowledge or a personal relationship with Target. The percentage of commission verses, however generally a broker will take around 5% to represent your product to Target.

We at Mr. Checkout have experience dealing with brokers and know there are several retail brokers that have poor business practices that can potentially damage your brand. If you are seeking a legitimate Target broker, please give us a call for a recommendation. It could save you a huge headache and a lot of money.

5. Complete the required Target paperwork.) Often Target will have you go through an application process. However, before submitting the paperwork required by Target, you should contact a buyer at Target and let them know your intentions. Having a contact inside of the company will potentially move your application more smoothly through the process.

6. Anticipate the need for increased volume.) Having Target agree to stock your product will most likely mean a significant increase in volume. You should be prepared to ramp up your production and inform your manufacturer of this opportunity.

Having production, logistics and distribution to sync is not only difficult; it requires a significant amount of time invested in customer relations. Also, Target may have stipulations in the contract that may penalize you for delays in shipping and production. Have an attorney explain all contracts to you if you don't understand the terms.

If you're looking to distribute your product to Target, be sure to assess the marketplace, carefully prepare for production growth thoroughly, and take full advantage of resources available to help you grow your business.

The process of selling your products in Target is somewhat different from the process you have to follow when selling your products in Walmart. Here are the steps you must follow to get the job done.

1.   Ask the right questions from yourself

The first step of selling, you should ask few questions from yourself. For example, you need to determine whether there is any demand for the products you offer or not. Then you need to get to know about the target market. You should also determine whether you are looking forward to selling what you got directly to Target, or you are just providing the license to the product, which can make them take care of distribution.

2. Be ready for the profits as well

You need to do an analysis beforehand to determine whether you are getting enough profits out of the product you sell on Target. The difference in between all associated expenses and price should be taken into consideration when calculating the profit.

In other words, the price tag of your product should be able to make you end up with a profit, after reducing the marketing, commission, shipping and packaging expenses. The product you offer should be worth your time and hassle as well. You are also encouraged to go through the pricing guidelines of Target, so that you will be able to get a better understanding about the other fees.

3. Pitch the product you have for Target

Once you are aware of the facts and are comfortable with selling on Target, you can go ahead and pitch your product to them. You will have to pitch your own product. Or else, you can get the assistance of a representative to get the job done. However, the exact presentation you prepare has the ability to help you with the results you end up with at the end of the day. Hence, you need to focus a lot on the strengths while you are pitching the product. You should also be aware about the questions that would come on your way. By preparing answers to those questions beforehand, you will be able to leave a lasting impression.

If you are not sure about confident pitching, you can get the help of a broker. The broker will charge a commission for pitching. However, the benefits you can get from the services of the broker are totally worth it when compared to the amount you spend.

4. Complete paperwork

Before you start selling on Target, you will be asked to go through an application process. However, you are not encouraged to go ahead and complete paperwork on your own. Instead, you are encouraged to get in touch with a buyer of Target and get to know about the intentions. When you are having a contact, you will find it as an easy task to complete the paperwork in a smooth manner.

5. Submit your paperwork

Once you are done with required paperwork, you can simply go ahead and submit it. After the submission, you will have to wait for about one week to get approved. Upon verification of required paperwork, you will be notified and you can simply go ahead and list your products.

6. Be ready for increase your volume

Surviving as a Target seller is never an easy thing to do. There are instances, where you will run out of stock. In other words, you will come across the need to increase your sales volume significantly. You need to be ready to face such situations as well. This can help you to deliver an impressive experience to your customers and take your selling efforts to the next level.

Now you have a clear understanding on what needs to be done in order to get your product to Target and Walmart. Hence, you can simply go ahead and start selling. The efforts you take to sell your products in Walmart or Target will be able to assist you with exciting results. However, you need to adhere to the rules and regulation of these platforms, especially if you want to go a long way with them.

Connect Americas

Connect Americas is a business portal with different resources to facilitate connection among businesses and governments from different countries in the Americas. Connect Americas was developed by the Inter-American Development Bank (IDB) and it receives support from Google, DHL, Visa and Alibaba.

It is easy to create a company profile and add your products at Connect Americas. The idea here is to seek business opportunities by bidding on requests posted on this website. You might find request like the following one "Calvo Conservas requires suppliers of glass bottles for food storage in Brazil." Login to Connect Americas account and click on Business Opportunities link to find opportunities and apply as a supplier. Some supplierd take care of the logistic aspect, so you only have to worry about selling.

When you try to apply for an business opportunity, Connect Americas will show the requirements for doing so. Do not be afraid to ask questions, there are many business opportunities you can win and you do not have to live in a particular country to win the contract. You can find information online and become an agent by selling someone else's product. In other words, a middleman between the producer and the buyer. Go to https://connectamericas.com and start making big money today.

GOVERNMENT CONTRACTING

"Government Contracts a Lesson in Patience." Here I will provide some tips in addition based on my experience in government contracting.

(1) A researcher wrote: "Although winning an initial contract can require more time, energy and money than some business owners can afford... [s]till, the federal government is an attractive source of money for many businesses that have lost private-sector work or clients... [use it] to counter the ebb and flow of their business...look hard at the federal market because it has money."

(2) Documentation is required to prove small-business eligibility and to obtain a number of certifications and registrations.

(a) Have a strategic plan of which government agencies you want to sell to.

(b) Submit your vendor registrations to your target agencies.

(c) Get any small business set aside certifications you are eligible for.

(d) Submit your certifications to your targeted agencies.

(3) Owners need to learn which agencies are best to target.

(a) Research which agencies are buying what you sell.

(i) Send your product and service codes (NAICS, PSC, FSC, NIGP) in a Capability Statement to the small business liaisons at the agencies and ask them if they have any requirements that you can help them with.

(ii) Search bid opportunities using search tools such as FBO.gov to find out which agencies are buying what you sell.

(4) Owners need to know how to write a government proposals.

(a) There is no bid proposal template because you need to follow the instructions in the solicitation.

(b) Also, pay close attention to the evaluation criteria used to rank bid proposals and to select contract awardees.

(5) Owners need to know how to network with procurement agents.

(a) Using your research about which agencies buy what you sell, start a contacts database.

(b) Create a Sales process - Systematically email, call, write and visit agency contacts that buy what you sell.

(c) Bid on jobs you can do as a prime or subcontractor.

(6) The process requires lots of patience.

(a) Learn the process slowly.

(b) Take a smaller job and don't get frustrated by the relatively small price tag of a first government assignment.

(7) You may have to rebrand your firm! Re-engineer!

(a) You want to be taken seriously as a government contractor.

(i) List your product and service codes, DUNs number, and CAGE number on all of your marketing materials and on your website.

(ii) List your small business certifications on all of your marketing materials and on your website.

(iii) List your vendor registrations on all of your marketing materials and on your website.

(iv) Mention any work you have done for government agencies in your marketing materials (include work you have done as a employee or another firm or government agency; include testimonials and references).

(v) If you have no government work experience, consider volunteering on a job to get experience that you can list in your marketing materials and on your website.

(b) You my have to tweak your business model.

(i) Use the research you have collected to consider whether there are products and services you should expand into or discontinue based on what you now know the government buys and sells.

(ii) But, be careful not to put all of your eggs in one basket - diversify and sell both to the private and public, government sector.

As you can surmise, you will indeed need patience to become a government contractor. The positioning, registrations, certifications, and marketing take time. But, keep your eyes on the prize. There are a number of small businesses making millions in the government contracting arena! So, all of the work necessary to lay the foundation can pay off!

GOVERNMENT CONTRACT PROPOSAL WRITING TIPS

Federal contracts are a very lucrative business. However, learning how to acquire projects takes time, effort and investment. Proposal writing for government contracts is by no means a simple process. However, if you attempt to respond to the agency's Request for Proposal (RFP), you will have to bring more to the table than just having a good technical writer. The reality is that the "status quo" no longer gets the win. You have to do more than the basic RFP requirements.

Agencies are now leaning towards trade-offs to justify their best value determinations. Lowest price does not necessarily get the award. As former government contracting officials and members of source selection teams, we have actually reviewed eloquent proposals and perfected efforts by technical writers - we know firsthand only the proposals that have substance and give the government added value and what source-selection officials want to know actually wins the contract. The agency wants to feel like it is getting a good deal - not just reviewing bids with the basic solicitation criteria.

Reasons Why Government Proposals Fail: The first thing to consider when responding to a multi-million dollar offer is whether you have the budget to do what it takes to win. Successful companies spend anywhere from $13K to $20K for proposal writing services for a contract valued anywhere from $1M-5M. Never just cut and paste old proposals for an upcoming project. Agencies spot templated responses from a mile away and automatically put your package proposal at the bottom of the pile.

When responding to a government Request for Proposal, we have found that the following summarizes why proposals fail.

1. The response is not specific and to the point. Government RFP preparation requires the bidder to articulate the key areas to the solicitation. Never try to write a book and expect the agency to understand what you are trying to say. Proposal writers must be very specific and to the point.

2. Too much focus on "we can do the work" instead of "how we are going to do the work." When grading proposals, the government places a significant emphasis and weight on the bidder's technical approach. You have to spell out HOW you actually perform each phase of the Statement of Work. Summarizing will not help you.

3. No emphasis on your risk management and quality assurance. One of the fatal mistakes in government contract proposal writing is that bidders miserably fail to address and highlight their risk management and quality assurance. The government is not going to award a contract worth millions and never pay attention to the risk involved. Each proposal writer who understands government contracting must include risk management into the response, to the solicitation. If you don't, then your competition certainly will.

4. Failure to understand best value considerations. In federal contracts, price alone is not the criteria for award and neither is past performance. Sometimes, agencies will consider a price/ past performance trade-off when considering awards. However, effective proposal writing includes more than just these factors. Congress has suggested that taxpayers' money should get the "best bang."

Since the government general buys commercial services and products, bidding on government contracts should incorporate factors commonly used in the commercial industry. This includes warranties, discounts for volume, accelerated schedules, etc. At Watson & Associates, our success stems from the ability to help you to see the big picture in federal procurement and educate the agency when writing government proposals.

5. Relying too heavily on teaming partners and subcontractors. Failure to understand that teaming rule can be the kiss of death in government proposal writing. Many companies that offer proposal writing services do not understand how to avoid this commonly-made mistake. Although FAR 9.6 allows for teaming and subcontracting, there are also limitations on subcontracting. When proposing a subcontractor or teaming partner, you have to understand the legal limitations.

Failure to correctly propose your team can subject you to a bid protest based upon affiliation. Bidding on government contracts means that the prime contractor (you) must perform the required percentage of labor costs and not pass through the critical aspects of the project. This is yet another reason why our experience as bid protest and government contract attorneys adds value to our proposal writing services.

As a general rule, there are ten basic principles that will put you on the right track to success in government RFP and proposal writing:

1. Always learn, learn and learn again the nature of the government's problem. If you cannot understand and respond to the agency's

problem, you simply will end up with an eloquently written document with no substance and lacking depth. The federal government publicizes its opportunities in a series of solicitations. As an effective proposal writer, you have to read, reread and understand the solicitation.

For example, average responses to a Request for Proposal (for medical supplies) simply inject paragraphs of how committed to customer service the bidder maybe; then, the bidder simply submits its pricing and past performance. The winning proposal uses a different strategy. Instead of drowning the RFP response with 'fluff', the experienced proposal consultant will advise his client to first discuss the industry and problems associated with this particular industry including problems experienced by other customers - this sets the stage for letting the government know you are ahead of the competition. You then describe how you can prevent these problems and describe what if anything you will do to minimize risk (this substantiates cost and shows additional value to the government.)

2. Never think that the government has no idea of what your service or product costs. Successful bidders understand the theory of the independent government estimate. The procurement rules require the government to establish some sort of estimate. Most agencies do their homework. However, some still use the outdated methodology that puts potential bidders at risk. Caution: The method arriving at the government estimate does not always work in your favor - the agency should conduct research in the commercial sector to see what similar products and services cost. Unfortunately, many agencies simply rely on other agency pricing to come up with the government estimate.

3. Always focus on beating your competitor. This is a mindset that swallows up inexperienced proposal writing staff. Many simply focus on responding to 'only what the solicitation calls for' and nothing more. At best, this line of thinking will get you within the competitive range, but not win you the award.

You always have to respond to the criteria accurately as set forth in the solicitation. However, this sets the stage (and a common trap) for only the basic requirements. Be mindful that your competition is also responding to the same RFP. You have to outperform them to get the award.

As you respond to each section of the RFP, always ask yourself, "what is your adversary going to write?" If you don't ask this question, you will undoubtedly find out during a debriefing of notice of non-selection for the bid.

4. For successful government proposal writing, you must have a thorough understanding of the procurement rules. To say otherwise is analogous to applying for a job at a large corporation without knowing anything about the company. Many companies hire proposal writers who have no clue, or even a basic understanding of the rules involved with procurement.

For example, many government contract proposals require you to discuss your teaming partners and subcontractors. More specifically, to discuss the roles and percentages of the contract. Many companies dive into this head-on without knowing the rules and laws of teaming and subcontracting. The result is many companies subject themselves to losing a bid protest for violation of the NAICS standards.

A second example is failure to understand the trade-off process. The contracting officer and the agency have wide discretion when determining what is a good deal for the government. When you fail to add more best-value considerations, you typically hand more discretion for trade-off determinations. If you don't give the agency something to consider, over and beyond price and past performance, your proposal will fail.

5. Unrealistic Proposal Pricing - Always be modest on profit. The old saying you can price yourself out of business applies to government contracting. As experienced proposal writing consultants, we advise our clients to stay within certain allowable percentages depending on the industry.

However, a good proposal writing strategy is to substantiate your pricing proposal by explaining critical processes and the costs associated with them. Assert common industry practice and justify your prices. Never allow the government to guess at why your pricing is high or low.

If you can compete with an extra low price, your proposal response should explain why your company can perform at such low prices. The solicitation may expressly state that too low of a price may indicate that you do not understand the proposal requirements. Do not give the government contracting department this luxury.

6. You must describe the 'horsepower' behind your company - Aka, Management Approach. This is a critical part of the proposal writing process. Successful bidders learn to how to write effective resumes specifically for federal RFPs. Simply put, traditional resumes don't lead to awards. The government wants in-depth information about the 'top brass' in your organization. Remember, technical proposals are weighted heavily when bidding on government contracts. Always talk about your key personnel, their experience and how they will participate in this government project.

7. In Government Proposal Writing never discuss your weaknesses. This is one of the most common traps in government contract proposal writing. When you see language in the solicitation asking you to describe past problems and how you handled them - warning, tread lightly.

For example, if you missed project schedules in a previous construction project, you may simply want to use another project for past performance and discuss it. The government does not want to award a construction project to a company with a history (even if only once) of missing deadlines.

The better proposal writing approach is to discuss potential problems in this specific project and then discuss how you intend to overcome them.

8. Never expect to get a million dollar contract for pennies. As mentioned proposal writing and development for a multi-million dollar contract is based upon a convincing RFP response. Bluntly put, a degree in English will not get you a multi-million dollar contract. You have to realistically budget for success. Although the skill of a technical writer is critical to the federal proposal writing

process, there is a huge difference - experience and knowledge of the rules.

9. Secure proposal writers who understand the procurement rules and the source selection process. This is a distinguishing factor when looking to hire a proposal development outsourcing staff.

10. Learn how to pick qualified proposal writers. The Internet is swamped with proposal writers for government contracts. However, picking the most qualified ones is the tricky part. Many shoppers typically want to know how many proposals a person has written in that specific industry; or what is their success rate.

To be frank - proposal writers do not have to be technically experienced in your industry. There are regulated rules in the bidding process. Understand those rules, trade-off strategies and how to present your package in a convincing manner are the cornerstones of bidding on federal government contracts.

When you are looking for **QUALIFIED PROPOSAL WRITER OR CONSULTANT**, here are relevant points to consider:

Level of experience in federal government contracting

- Have them describe important issues when writing about best value
- The level of experience they have in responding to government RFPs that involve teaming partners or subcontractors
- Ask what does the government need to know about a prospective bidder to set a high impression

Understand that prior win rates do not guarantee a win in this effort. Most businesses seek proposal writers based on their win rates - only to lose in this particular effort. As government contract lawyers, we also get the same question - what is your win rate? Not only is this misleading but the analysis and inference of prior win rates can be negative. The question to ask is how would you guide my company into possibly winning this project?

Each RFP is unique and the focus must be specific to the proposal at hand - how are you going to attack the solicitation and submit a winning proposal on THIS project?

- Agencies look for different things in their solicitations

- Not all agencies follow the FAR (See FDIC)

- Rating criteria is different in virtually all RFPs

- Lowest price (alone) is not the statutory requirement for award in federal contracts

- High- Caliber Advice Sets You Apart from Your Competitors

As you venture into the market for a government contract proposal writing consultant, you are investing in someone who can convince the government you are the best candidate for award. This is a skill that goes over and beyond proofreading and editing. Proposal writers must understand and have experience in the actual rules of engagement and the pitfalls associated with losing an award on a bid protest. This foresight sets you apart from your competitors and automatically increases your caliber and probabilities of being successful.

GUIDES FOR OBTAINING GSA CONTRACTS

General Service Administration (GSA) contracts benefit the federal government and the companies that supply it with products and services. For the government, the contracts deliver products and services at preferred prices. For companies, they offer a steady stream of revenue, and make it easier to set financial goals. Because the contracts are negotiated directly with the government, the bidding process is eliminated, saving the government and the companies it buys from valuable time.

GSA contracts are not difficult to obtain when a company has the right information and takes the right steps. If your company plans to apply for a contract, the tips below will help it succeed:

Understand the Offerings of Competitors

According to GSA consulting firms, understanding the offerings of competitors is one of the most important steps to obtaining a contract. Most companies are aware of competition in the regular market, but they are not as well acquainted with competition in the federal market. Understanding competition in the federal market helps a company present a unique case for its offerings, which makes it easier for agencies to assess the value of the offerings.

Exhibit at Agency Events

Exhibiting goods or services at federal conventions and tradeshows is an excellent way for companies to gain exposure to federal customers. Meeting federal buyers may also result in sales. At the least, it creates a dialogue between the company and its potential customers that informs the company what agencies to target with a GSA proposal.

Choose the right SINs

Special Item Numbers (SINs) are listed in the Request For Proposal (RFP) for a GSA Schedule. In many cases, a company could target its proposal toward several SINs, but the key is to find SINs that fit the product or service best, as this makes it easier for the contract officer to assess the proposal. GSA consulting firms offer valuable advice for choosing the right SINs.

Create a succinct proposal

GSA contracts are won by succinct proposals meeting the GSA's informational and formatting requirements. The administration establishes a limit for the length of proposals, but constructing the shortest proposal possible is a good idea. The easier it is for a contract officer to evaluate the proposal, the greater the chance that the proposal will receive an accurate response.

Check for RFP Updates

The GSA regularly updates RFP information. In many cases, the updates change the way companies apply for contracts. When an RFP update is made, companies have a thirty-day grace period to submit a proposal under the previous RFP rules. Considering that many proposals take longer than thirty days to research and compose, companies should check for RFP updates before they begin drafting the proposal.

Conclusion

GSA contracts allow companies to sell goods and services in the federal marketplace. The tips above are useful information for companies that are planning to pursue a contract. In most situations, companies have the greatest chance of securing a contract when they use the services of GSA consulting firms.

HOW TO GET A GSA SCHEDULE CONTRACT AND SELL TO THE GOVERNMENT

Learning how to get a GSA Schedule contract is an important step for maximum profit from supplying products or services to the government of the United States. A GSA Government contract can not only present you with multiple federal business opportunities through the various products distributed by the General Services Administration, it can also open other doors for your business with government agencies other than the GSA.

While qualifications for each Schedule Contract within the General Services Administration may vary and mandate more than the basic qualifications, these are the minimum requirements your company must meet to sell to the government with the GSA:

- Any felonies found in chief officers of your company within three (3) years of seeking a GSA Contract will render your company disqualified

- The service or product for which you are seeking a GSA Schedule Contract must be currently sold on the open market

- Your business must have a minimum live history of two (2) years and be able to prove a minimum gross sales volume of twenty-five thousand dollars ($25,000.00) for two (2) consecutive years

If your company meets the basic criteria, it may be worth your while to take the next steps in learning how to get a GSA Contract.

GSA Schedules

The General Services Administration offers a wide range of products which are categorized by Schedules and SIN'S. There are around forty (40) GSA Schedules with somewhat broad category definitions, such as: Publication Media, Logistics Worldwide,

Environmental Services, Medical and Dental Equipment, Logistics, Engineering, and more. Within each Schedule is a list of Item numbers which are individually referred to as a SIN (Special Item Number). The SIN is a more specific indication of the types of products or services offered within each Schedule.

The first step in applying for a GSA Schedule Contract is to identify the most applicable Schedule(s) and SIN(s) for your company. Although your business may offer services from multiple GSA Schedules, you must be sure to carefully review the qualifications for each schedule to ensure your business meets all listed criteria.

If you find that multiple Schedule Contracts are available to your business, you can either submit applications for multiple schedules or focus on one at a time to slowly introduce yourself to federal procurement, carefully building a solid past performance record. You can find out what government Agencies are spending in your specific Schedule by visiting the GSA website and library to determine the most profitable prospect if you are interested in seeking one Contract within each Schedule at a time.

If you are having trouble identifying the most applicable Schedule to your business, you may contact a GSA Representative to provide clarification. It's important to remember representatives are available to help you with the entire process. Although some business owners prefer to outsource GSA Services for lack of time or reduction of stress, a business owner who is willing to dedicate the time and focus can save money by personally learning how to get a GSA Schedule Contract and taking the steps necessary to be awarded a contract with the General Services Administration.

Certification, Registration, and Documentation

Inevitably upon reviewing the requirements for your targeted GSA Schedule Contract, you will find there are additional registrations and certifications your business needs. Aside from final mandatory registrations and certifications, you will need to prepare copies of all your other registrations and prepare in the format indicated in your Schedule Contract guidelines to go with your bid.

Preparing a Bid for a GSA Schedule Contract

Preparing a bid for a GSA Schedule Contract is a delicate process which consists of due diligence, analyzing financials, and identifying and outlining all relevant details of your business. There are a few very important points to consider when applying for a GSA Schedule Contract...

Lower Cost and Higher Volume

One of the biggest advantages of the General Services Administration to world-wide customers in both the private sector and government agencies is the low prices offered on major acquisitions. If you are not able to offer significantly lower prices than you currently do on the goods or services offered by your business for government contracts ranging from twenty-five thousand dollars ($25,000.00) to one million dollars ($1,000,000.00) or more while still earning a profit, the GSA may not be an ideal distribution channel for your company.

It will be important for you to know your bottom line on delivery of goods and develop a pricing structure which will allow your business to offer competitive rates through the General Services Administration while relying on the volume of federal acquisition to generate revenue.

Relevant Detailed Capabilities Statement

A capabilities statement or an equivalent document will be required on your GSA Schedule Contract Application. You will want to provide only relevant information to the Schedule for which you are applying and provide as comprehensible of details as possible when outlining the specialties or your business and the services or goods you offer.

Regularly Review Schedule Guidelines

Federal procurement laws change regularly, and the General Services Administration sometimes updates its Schedule Guidelines along with various procedures and trading standards. It is important to check back with the GSA on a regular basis while constructing your Schedule Contract bid to ensure you have the most updated list of criteria and submission requirements.

Submitting a GSA Schedule Contract Application

Depending on the GSA Schedule under which you are seeking a contract, approval time can range between three (3) and nine (9) months. Submission of a GSA Schedule Contract is not necessarily the final step before being awarded a contract by the General Services Administration. It is important to follow up with your Schedule Contract application and stay aware of updates to the GSA pertaining to your schedule.

There are a variety of reasons why your application will need to be modified, and if you maintain regular contact with a representative and stay informed of GSA updates you can keep your application current and increase your company's odds of contract approval.

Acquiring a GSA Contract may not be an easy process, but the prospect of selling to the government at the level at which the GSA operates is a promising end to validate the means. If you find you meet the basic qualifications for conducting business with the General Services Administration, you can either invest monetarily in GSA Services or invest the time yourself by learning how to get a GSA Schedule Contract.

The United States Government spends over five hundred billion dollars ($500,000,000,000.00) every year contracting with companies in the private sector. Increase your odds of selling to the government by earning a contract award from the General Services Administration.

HOW TO WIN A GOVERNMENT CONTRACT

Does your business qualify for a government contract? Many business owners avoid government contracting for a number of reasons including, but not limited to, excessive documentation, stringent financial reviews and the general complexities associated with federal and state contracts. As a result, many business owners (about 80% of the nation's small businesses) do not participate in this trillion dollar industry.

Anybody who has ever attempted to investigate government contracting at the federal level is keenly aware of the myriad details and bureaucratic nightmare and the volume of information that must be absorbed before an individual can even begin to make sense of how the system works. Frankly, it is bizarre. The people who work for the governments (local, state and federal) simply have too much time on their hands to develop rules, regulations, policies and procedures and a document for everything. Who has the time or inclination to muddle through all this complexity to bid on a highly competitive contracting process, which you will probably not win anyway? That's a good question and here are some answers.

Getting a government contract, while highly competitive, will probably not create a windfall stream of revenue for your business, but it will produce a steady stream which you can be assured of timely payment and, the revenue can be directly applied to cover your overhead. This will allow you to achieve economies of scale that enable you to win more profitable commercial contracts in the private sector. It also adds market credibility with your customers when they know you are substantial enough to service a government contract whether it is a local, state or federal contract.

Most people think of the feds when they think of government contracting. But there are many purchases made by local and state governments, which your small business may be very well qualified to compete. Your local government purchases many things not normally considered: everything from bathroom supplies to car leases, audiovisual equipment and janitorial services. The local government should be your first target for winning a contract less than $25,000.00. It is recommended to start with a small contract until you get familiarized with the process.

And that is the key to success: One thing the various levels of government look for is a track record with commercial customers. They want to know they are contracting with a business that can indeed deliver the contracted goods and services. And the best way you can gain credibility with the government is to start small and build a track record. How? Sell to townships and small cities or county governments within your state and be successful at servicing your customers well with emphasis on customer service.

Their testimonials will carry a lot of weight with each successive small government you bid to contract with. You build this reputation layer by layer from the ground up. You can't get the big things done until you get the little things done first, right? So, start small and contact your county to find out how the bidding process works in your area.

Whether you are planning to seek government contracts at the local, state or federal level, or private contracts, it makes sense to see the acquisition process through the eyes of the purchasing agent/authority who will be making the decision to award the contract. There are three basic points to consider that a purchasing agent definitely considers: Planning, Participation, and Protection:

PLANNING: Contracting procurement officers (CPOs) and purchasing agents (PAs) often rely upon the department, agency or institution for input regarding an acquisition planning and will consider a variety of issues that help identify the minimum needs of the agency or the end user. This information is used in the planning phase and the development of the request for proposal (RFP).

PARTICIPATION: After the planning and needs analysis, the development of the RFP is many times a collaborative effort with specifications provided by a person or team of experts who have carefully thought through the technical aspects of the acquisition. This technical information is used to develop the RFP for release to the bidding market. CPOs or PAs will identify existing specifications based on internal needs and, depending on the size and scope of the acquisition project, an exhaustive market research.

The point is that purchasing agents do their homework before they release the RFP and they know a lot about the industry/commercial sector and have intelligent expectations of market costs and services revolving around their potential purchase.

PROTECTION: CPOs and PAs want protection before they award a contract to any bidding party. The first thing they consider is the past performance of the bidding companies and the winning company's ability to satisfy all requirements of the contract at the absolute best possible price, with the best possible terms, service and warranty combination. They want protection and they know how to get it through the competitive bidding process.

I have been involved in government bidding a few times and there are pros and cons associated with the process. The "pros" of the process is to win a contract and enjoy the revenue stream that results therefrom. The "cons" are that a hell of a lot of hard work can go into the bidding process without a payoff. One bidding situation I was involved in was with a state agency taking bids on a creative job placement process to help people with disabilities gain employment with a living wage.

There were about 100 organizations involved with the bid and each organization came up with the best pitch, price service and performance angle. We did not win the bid. But what the state got, was 100 sources of free ideas from business in the field of marketing, job placement, advertising, etc., and it didn't cost the state a dime.

If those same 100 businesses were contacted and PAID for their input, it would have cost the state a TON for the professional advice and ideas they received through the bidding war. The state really worked the crowd and milked 99 companies for the strategic information that was, presumably, kept by the state and handed over to the winning company to incorporate the best ideas into the entire job placement system. It was a sleazy deal and convinced me to stray away from any further "creative idea type proposals" with any organization, especially the government. Just a point to ponder...

There is money and revenue stability in government contracts for those with the capacity to deliver goods and services. As I said in (part 1) of this mini series, it makes sense to build up a track record (past performance) by bidding on projects in your own backyard with villages, townships, small cities and counties before going after the big fish at the state and fed level. Although, going for smaller grants is not a prerequisite to pursuing state and federal contracts it does build experience with the process.

CONTRACT CASE STUDIES

The following cases can serve to study and learn about the problem and how would you approach the problem to solve it. The cases are to give you some ideas that small businesses have the opportunity to compete and win government contracts, but they have to make sure to deliver on the contract requirements. If the requirements are not met, the contract will be voided and the government could ban you from submitting future bidding:

- Whitefish Energy - $300 million for Puerto Rico power grid restoration. http://fortune.com/2017/10/25/puerto-rico-whitefish-power-grid/

- Tribute Contracting - 30 million meals to Puerto Rico. https://www.huffingtonpost.com/entry/fema-contractor-failed-to-deliver-millions-of-meals-to-puerto-rico-lawmakers_us_5a7a0d40e4b06505b4e8cfbe

- David Packouz and Efraim Diveroli - $300 million arm deal. https://www.motherjones.com/politics/2015/06/b00k-arms-dudes-guy-lawson-pentagon-contracting/

SUMMARY

Do not spend much time working on your website, if more of your sales are coming from other sources. More likely Google will not give you a good ranking on your website even if you pay a Search Engine Optimisation (SEO) guru. Instead, focus on increasing sales where you can get a better return. Groupon and Amazon are good places to sale and have a good stream of incoming in your bank account every 15 days while eBay can provide you the same day cash when you need immediate fund to cover some expenses.

EBay's buyers love free shipping and lower prices on items. It's not hard to get the hot item symbol of on your product on eBay, but it will go away if you make changes to your listing. Do not change your listing after it starts getting popular on eBay.

If you get your product on a major retail store, help your product get more exposure by promoting it and make it become popular so it sells faster. The result will help you to get a larger order from the store when they submit their next order. We gave you ideas and places where to sell your products, but you do not have to focus on all of them. You can start with popular online marketplaces until you get a larger order from a retail store or the government.

So we've covered how to find your product, how to source it, how to send it into Amazon, set up your listing, optimize that listing and get sales.

That covers how to launch a product on Amazon. In order to scale your business, you just follow and repeat that process by launching more and more products. I hope that breaks down the process for you and you're excited to start your own business on Amazon.

If you'd like any further information on any of the topic you read on this book, or to get updated content of this beBook, visit our community page at https://TuOpinion.org.

www.ingramcontent.com/pod-product-compliance
Lightning Source LLC
Chambersburg PA
CBHW030014190526
45157CB00016B/2697